I Like Jam

by Betsy Franco
illustrated by Jackie Snider

Copyright © by Harcourt, Inc.

All rights reserved. No part of this publication may be reproduced or transmitted in any form or by any means, electronic or mechanical, including photocopy, recording, or any information storage and retrieval system, without permission in writing from the publisher.

Requests for permission to make copies of any part of the work should be mailed to the following address: School Permissions, Harcourt, Inc., 6277 Sea Harbor Drive, Orlando, Florida 32887-6777.

HARCOURT and the Harcourt Logo are trademarks of Harcourt, Inc.

Printed in the United States of America

ISBN 0-15-317201-0 – I Like Jam

Ordering Options
ISBN 0-15-318588-0 (Package of 5)
ISBN 0-15-316985-0 (Grade 1 Package)

3 4 5 6 7 8 9 10 179 02 01 00

My name is Joey,
And I like jam.
My mom likes soup.
My dad likes ham.

Bats like bugs,
And horses like oats.
You can give all that
And more to goats.

A kangaroo likes grass.
It does. I know!
And a snail likes vegetables—
Any kind I grow!

Would a cat that's wild
Like to get a pig?
And does a caterpillar
Like a fig?

My dog likes what I like.
She gets her wish!
And a shark will eat
Any kind of fish.

See, I like jam
So I sit by the door
Because I want
To eat some more!

Here comes my jam.
It fills all of these bags!
I'll soon be eating some
With my dog, Rags!

I like jam,
As you can see.
If you like jam,
Come eat with me!

Teacher/Family Member

Jam Jar
Have children draw a large jam jar on a piece of paper. Ask them to fill the jar with pictures of things *they* like to eat.

 School-Home Connection

Invite your child to read *I Like Jam* to you. Help your child find all of the rhyming words in the poem. Then take turns reading the verses.

Word Count:	136	
Vocabulary Words:	any	because
	kind	soon
	door	
Phonic Elements:	Long Vowel: /ō/ *ow, oa*	
	oats	know
	goats	grow

TAKE-HOME BOOK
Bright Ideas
Use with "The Fox and the Stork" and
"The Very Boastful Kangaroo."